The Foolish Hare and The Mango Tree

by Narinder Dhami
Illustrated by Silvia Provantini

Contents

The Foolish Hare 2
The Mango Tree 25

The Foolish Hare

Long ago, Hari the hare was fast asleep underneath a palm tree. His whiskers trembled and his nose twitched because he was having a terrible nightmare. Hari was dreaming that the sky was falling down. The sun had disappeared, and the trees were toppling. It felt like the world was coming to an end.

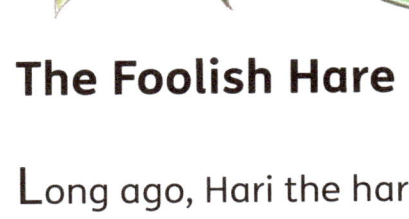

Hari woke up with a start. He was very relieved to find that it had all been a dream.

"What a horrible nightmare!" he muttered. "What would happen to me if the sky really did fall down?"

Little did Hari know that he was being watched …

High above Hari's head, a troop of monkeys was hiding among the leaves. They had heard every word Hari said, and they started chuckling.

"What a foolish hare!" one monkey sneered. "He was only dreaming, but he's still worried about the sky falling down."

"I've got a brilliant idea!" the biggest monkey said with a grin. "Let's play a trick on him!"

The monkey searched around until he found an enormous coconut. He pulled the coconut off its stem and let it plummet to the ground behind the palm tree.

The coconut hit the ground with an ear-splitting crack and burst open. On the other side of the tree, Hari was so shocked that he almost jumped out of his furry skin!

"It wasn't a dream!" Hari gasped in horror. "A piece of the sky has fallen down. If the rest of the sky falls down too, then the world is <u>bound</u> to come to an end ... HELP!"

The naughty monkeys peered down from the tree and stuffed their paws into their mouths to stop their laughter.

Hari said, "... the world is <u>bound</u> to come to an end." Does this mean he thought it would definitely happen, or that it might happen?

"I must warn the other hares that the sky is falling down!" Hari cried. He didn't stop to check what had made the loud cracking sound. He simply raced off in a panic.

The monkeys watched him go and roared with laughter until their sides hurt. Then they climbed down the tree to feast on the broken pieces of coconut on the ground.

Hari charged through the jungle. He was so upset, he didn't see Meena hopping towards him. Hari bumped right into her. Meena was <u>furious</u>.

"Well, that's a nice way to treat your best friend!" she snapped. "Why are you running so fast? Is a wolf chasing you?"

Can you do an impression of Meena being <u>furious</u> with Hari?

"No," Hari gasped. "The sky is falling down!"

"Are you sure?" Meena asked, trembling with fright.

"I heard a giant crack, louder than any clap of thunder," Hari told her. "Soon the rest of the sky will fall down, the sun will disappear, and the world will come to an end!"

"We must tell everyone!" Meena cried.

Together, Hari and Meena raced off to warn the other hares.

"The sky is falling down!" they both shouted. "We must escape and find somewhere safe to hide! Run for your lives!"

The other hares began popping up out of the long grass, looking very frightened.

"Hurry!" Hari and Meena yelled. "We must get away before the rest of the sky falls down on us!"

Soon all the terrified hares were running away in a panic.

A herd of deer was grazing peacefully on the lush green grass. The deer raised their heads and stared in amazement as the hares rushed past.

"What's happening?" one of the deer called.

"The sky is falling down!" the last hare explained. "We're searching for a safe place to hide."

The deer glanced at each other in terror.

"We must get away from here, too!" one of them decided. "Quick, follow the hares!"

"Where are we running to?" a baby deer asked, but no one answered.

 The hares went racing off into the distance, and the herd of deer dashed after them. They all hurtled along in a panic calling out, "The sky is falling down! Run for your lives!"

 A black bear, who was asleep in his den, was woken by the noise.

"What's going on?" the bear roared. "I'm trying to sleep!"

"The sky is falling down!" one of the deer called. "Run away with us and find a safe place to hide!"

The bear couldn't believe his ears.

"I'll tell the other bears!" he roared. "We're coming with you!"

Soon, a crowd of black bears was chasing after the hares and the deer. Puffing and panting, they all rushed on and on until they came to a crystal-clear lake. A herd of elephants was bathing in the lake, playfully spraying each other with water.

As the long line of animals snaked around the edge of the lake, the elephants gazed at them in astonishment.

"What's happening?" one of the elephants asked.

"Don't you know? The sky is falling down!" a bear panted. "You should leave straight away and follow us to safety!"

The elephants were immediately panic-stricken.

"We need to save ourselves before the sky falls down!" the leader of the herd trumpeted. "Follow the bears!"

The elephants lumbered out of the lake and stampeded after the bears, the deer and the hares.

A lion was strolling along, enjoying the sunshine. Suddenly, he heard a sound like thunder. The earth trembled beneath his paws.

As the sound grew louder, the lion looked up with alarm. His eyes widened as he watched the hares, deer, bears and elephants charging straight towards him.

"**STOP!**" the lion roared in his loudest voice.

All of the animals immediately skidded to a halt, bumping into each other. The lion was king of the jungle, and everyone feared him.

"Tell me, where are you all running to?" asked the lion.

"Your Majesty, the sky is falling down!" the leader of the elephants told him. "We're going to hide in a safe place."

"The sky is falling down?" the lion repeated with a frown. "I <u>refuse</u> to believe that. Who told you such nonsense?"

"They did!" all the elephants said together, pointing their trunks at the black bears.

"It's true!" the bears cried.

"This sounds like a very silly story!" the lion growled softly. "Who told you?"

The lion <u>refused</u> to believe the sky was falling down. What else could he have said instead of "I <u>refuse</u> ..."?

"They did!" the bears muttered, nodding towards the herd of deer. The deer looked embarrassed.

"The hares said the sky was falling down and that we had to escape," one deer mumbled.

The lion turned to the hares. "Who told you that?" he asked.

"He did!" the hares shouted, glaring at Hari.

"It's true, Your Majesty," Hari said. "I was asleep under a tree, and I dreamt that the sky was falling down. Then I woke up and heard a loud crack. The sky really is falling down!"

"I require proof of this story," the lion said sternly. "Take me to this tree."

Why do you think the lion required proof of the story?

The monkeys were lazing around in the palm tree when suddenly they felt the ground begin to shake. Alarmed, they peered through the leaves and saw hares, deer, bears, elephants and a lion racing towards them.

One by one, the monkeys tumbled out of the tree and down to the ground.

"Monkeys!" the lion said grimly. "I should have guessed!"

The lion padded behind the tree and discovered the pieces of coconut shell.

"This coconut made the noise you heard," he told Hari.

"So the sky isn't falling down?" Hari asked, relieved.

"No," the lion replied. "Next time, make sure of the facts before you run around telling stories!" He glared at the monkeys and let out an enormous roar. "And no more tricks! Hari could have been knocked <u>unconscious</u>!"

The monkeys screeched in terror and scampered away.

If Hari had been knocked <u>unconscious</u>, would he have been awake or in a deep sleep?

The Mango Tree

Once upon a time, a beautiful mango tree grew straight and tall in an Indian field. The mango tree had a broad trunk, curved branches and glossy, green leaves.

The only problem was that the tree had never borne fruit. So Ifran, the owner of the field, was delighted when one year he saw plump mangoes hanging from the branches for the very first time.

The mango tree had a broad trunk. Can you imagine what the trunk looked like? What other word could you use to describe the trunk that has the same meaning as 'broad'?

"I can hardly wait to taste my very first mango!" Ifran thought.

He began to inspect the fruit. A few of the mangoes were still green and not yet ready to eat, but most of them were beautifully ripe and golden yellow.

Ifran found a juicy-looking mango. He was about to pick it when a furious voice yelled: "STOP!"

Can you think of a word that means the opposite of 'furious'?

Surprised, Ifran spun around. His neighbour, Abu, was rushing across the field towards him.

"Why are you stealing my mangoes, Ifran?" Abu asked, angrily.

Ifran was shocked. "Your mangoes?" he said, with a gasp. "Abu, this is my mango tree! It's right here on the edge of my field."

"It's on the edge of my field, too!" Abu pointed out.

"I planted the mango seed right here, Abu!" Ifran argued. "You must have seen me watering the young tree as it grew!"

"No, I planted the mango seed in this very spot!" Abu declared. "I cared for it every day. That's why the tree is so tall and strong!"

The two men glared at each other.

"Look, it's almost night," Ifran said. The sun was going down, painting the sky with pink and gold. "Let's go home, and we can talk about this again tomorrow."

"I <u>refuse</u> to go anywhere!" Abu snapped, folding his arms. "Do you think I'm a fool? If I go home, you'll steal all my ripe mangoes!"

Why did Abu <u>refuse</u> to go home?

"We can share the mangoes," Ifran offered.

Abu shook his head. "I'm not sharing with anyone!" he said firmly.

"Very well," Ifran sighed. "Then we must go and visit Birbal, the wisest man in the land. He'll decide which one of us owns this beautiful mango tree."

Abu nodded. "Let's leave first thing tomorrow."

The next morning, Ifran and Abu went to visit Birbal, the wise man. Birbal lived at the royal palace of the Emperor Akbar, and he was famous for being both clever and fair-minded.

When Ifran and Abu arrived at the palace, there was a crowd of people waiting to see Birbal. Ifran and Abu joined the queue.

After a long, hot wait, it was finally Ifran and Abu's turn.

"Good morning, friends," Birbal said, with a smile. "Now, what do you require from me?"

"Sir, I have a beautiful mango tree on the edge of my field," Ifran began.

"No, the tree is on the edge of my field!" Abu butted in.

Birbal said, "Now, what do you require from me?" What other word could he have used instead of 'require'?

"I planted the mango seed," said Ifran.

"No, I planted the seed!" Abu argued.

"I watered the seed every day," Ifran said loudly.

"I cared for the mango tree!" Abu yelled.

"So," said Birbal firmly, "you want me to decide who is the rightful owner of the mango tree?"

"Yes please, sir!" Ifran and Abu said together.

Birbal took a sip of water and frowned. "I need more time to think about this," he said. "Go home and return here tomorrow for my answer."

"Tomorrow!" Abu gasped in dismay.

"Thank you, sir," Ifran said, gratefully. "We shall see you tomorrow morning."

Ifran and Abu turned to leave.

"I can't believe we have to wait until tomorrow!" Abu grumbled, as they walked to the palace gates. "Maybe Birbal isn't so wise after all!"

Ifran said nothing. He was sure they could trust Birbal to do the right thing.

They didn't know that Birbal was watching them both closely.

Birbal waited until Ifran and Abu had gone. Then he called for Casper, one of his most trusted servants.

"Casper, I have a <u>task</u> for you. Do you see those two men in the gardens?" Birbal asked, looking at Ifran and Abu. "I want you to follow them to their homes. Then …" Birbal whispered his orders into Casper's ear.

Birbal had a <u>task</u> for Casper. What did he want Casper to do first? What was the last <u>task</u> you had to do?

Casper darted out of the palace and down the broad marble steps. He could see Ifran and Abu not far ahead of him. They were just leaving through the tall golden gates. Casper hurried to catch up with them. Then, keeping the men in sight, he followed them into the busy streets of the city.

Very soon, Ifran and Abu left the city behind and began walking along the bumpy, dusty track that led to their farms. Casper wasn't far behind them. He could hear that Ifran and Abu were still arguing about the mango tree.

"Birbal is <u>bound</u> to decide that the tree belongs to me!" Abu boasted.

"We'll see," Ifran replied.

Abu boasted that Birbal was <u>bound</u> to decide the tree belonged to him. Does this mean Abu thought Birbal would definitely decide the tree belonged to him, or that he wasn't sure?

Soon they reached a fork in the road. Ifran went one way and Abu the other. Casper decided to follow Ifran home first. He waited until Ifran had gone inside and closed the door. Then he ran into the yard and began knocking and banging at the door and yelling Ifran's name.

"Ifran! Ifran!" Casper shouted. "You must come quickly!"

Ifran opened the door and frowned. "Who are you, and why are you banging on my door?" he asked.

Casper repeated what Birbal had told him to say.

"Ifran, some of the poor people from the village nearby are stealing your ripe mangoes!" Casper said. "They are starving!"

"Oh dear," Ifran sighed. "They must be very hungry. Never mind, there are enough mangoes for everyone. I don't want them to suffer." He smiled at Casper. "Thank you for telling me."

Then Casper dashed off to Abu's house. There, he did exactly the same thing. He knocked and banged at the door, shouting, "Abu! You need to come right away! There are people stealing your mangoes!"

Ifran didn't want people to suffer from hunger. What does that tell you about him?

Abu flung the door open with a crash.

"Stealing my mangoes?" he roared. "How dare they!"

"It's the poor people from the nearby village," Casper explained. "They're starving."

Abu didn't care. He was furious! Grabbing a broom, he raced out of the yard.

"I'll teach them a lesson!" he yelled, waving the broom in the air.

Casper hurried back to the royal palace. There he found Birbal playing chess with Emperor Akbar. Quickly, Casper explained to Birbal what had happened.

"I understand," Birbal said, nodding his head. Then he moved one of his chess pieces. "Checkmate!" he said and smiled at the emperor. "I win again."

"You're too clever for me, Birbal!" the emperor laughed.

The following day, Ifran and Abu returned to the palace where Birbal was waiting for them.

"I have decided we shall split the tree in half!" Birbal announced. "You will each get an equal share of the mangoes. Then the tree trunk will be chopped in half with an axe, and the wood will be shared equally, too."

"If we must, sir," Abu muttered grumpily. He'd hoped to get the whole tree. At least he'd have mangoes to eat and plenty of firewood for the winter.

Ifran had tears in his eyes.

"Sir," he said softly, "the tree is a living thing, and I can't see it suffer. Please don't split it in half. Abu can have it!"

Birbal nodded.

"Ifran, you're a very kind man," he said. "You have proved to me who really owns the mango tree. The tree is yours!"

"Sir ..." Abu spluttered angrily.

"Did you really plant a mango seed, Abu?" Birbal asked sternly.

"Yes, sir," Abu mumbled. "However, I forgot to water it, and it died!"

"We can share the mangoes," Ifran offered kindly, and Abu's face lit up.

"Thank you," he said. "I'm sorry I pretended the mango tree was mine."

Birbal smiled. "Just remember this, Abu. It is much better to be kind than it is to be greedy!"

Read and discuss

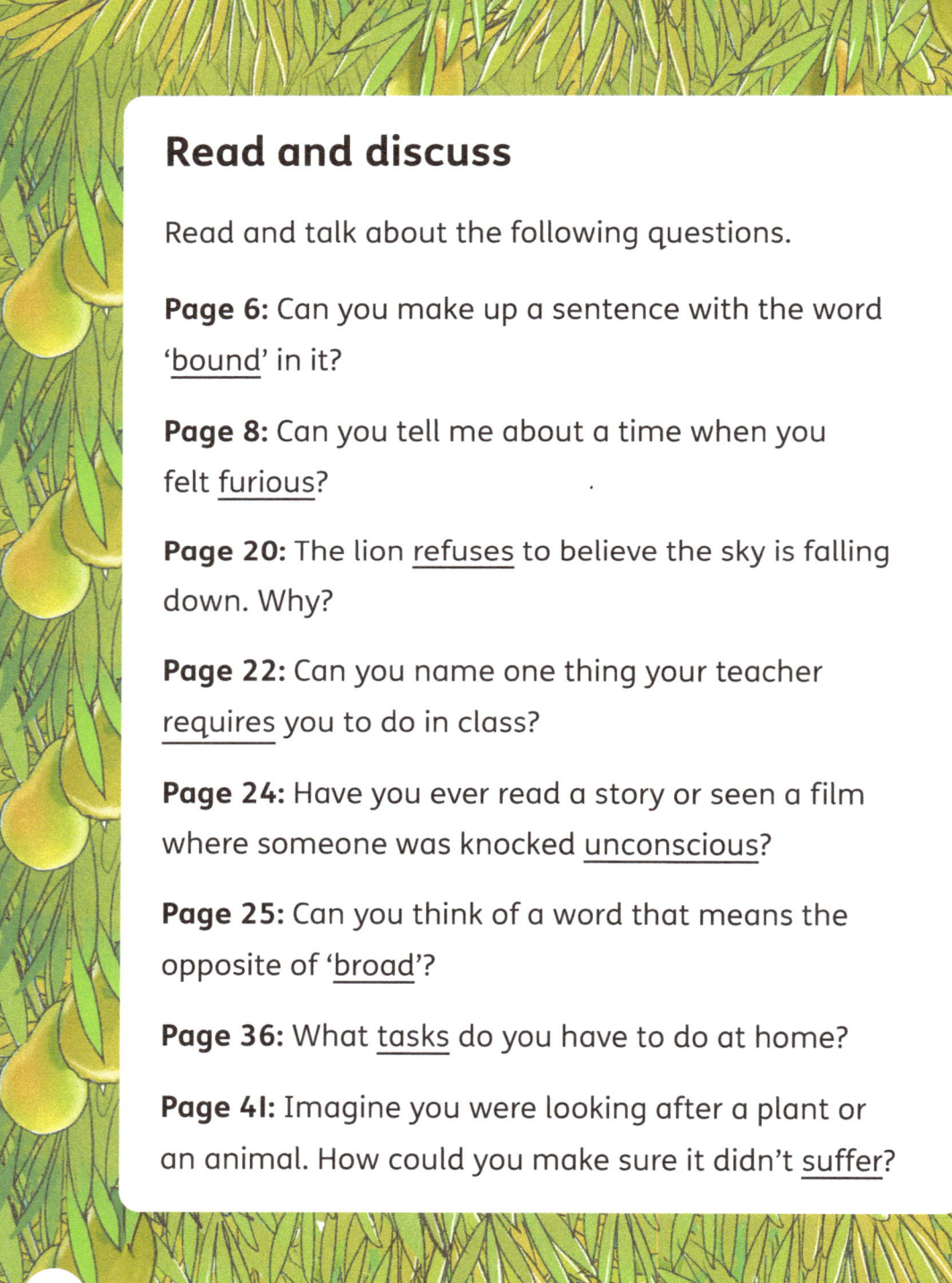

Read and talk about the following questions.

Page 6: Can you make up a sentence with the word 'bound' in it?

Page 8: Can you tell me about a time when you felt furious?

Page 20: The lion refuses to believe the sky is falling down. Why?

Page 22: Can you name one thing your teacher requires you to do in class?

Page 24: Have you ever read a story or seen a film where someone was knocked unconscious?

Page 25: Can you think of a word that means the opposite of 'broad'?

Page 36: What tasks do you have to do at home?

Page 41: Imagine you were looking after a plant or an animal. How could you make sure it didn't suffer?